# JAPANESE DESIGNS
## Coloring Book

### Y. S. GREEN

DOVER PUBLICATIONS, INC.
Mineola, New York

# Introduction

By presenting this delightful array of traditional Japanese designs, artist Y. S. Green has provided enchanting views of the decorative arts in Japan during several centuries. With unerring skill, she has exquisitely redrawn each carefully selected motif for coloring.

Among the thirty designs presented are images of cranes and carp, rabbits and a tortoise, cherry and plum blossoms, chrysanthemums and camellias, butterflies and dragonflies, bamboo leaves and maple leaves, as well as a host of other floral and botanical motifs. A dragon, a Chinese lion, and a pair of phoenixes are featured in this marvelous collection, as are several symbols of longevity. Also included are decorated fans and basketry.

The distinctive designs originally were created during various periods of Japanese cultural history for clothing, other textiles, lacquerware, and ceramics. Together, they provide a series of windows through which to view Japanese artistic themes and styles.

*Bibliographical Note*

*Japanese Designs Coloring Book* is a new work, first published by Dover Publications, Inc., in 2002.

DOVER *Pictorial Archive* SERIES

This book belongs to the Dover Pictorial Archive Series. You may use the designs and illustrations for graphics and crafts applications, free and without special permission, provided that you include no more than four in the same publication or project. (For permission for additional use, please write to Permissions Department, Dover Publications, Inc., 31 East 2nd Street, Mineola, N.Y. 11501.)

However, republication or reproduction of any illustration by any other graphic service, whether it be in a book or in any other design resource, is strictly prohibited.

*International Standard Book Number: 0-486-42377-8*

Manufactured in the United States of America
Dover Publications, Inc., 31 East 2nd Street, Mineola, N.Y. 11501

Cranes, irises, maple leaves, and a wave motif: from a nineteenth-century textile.

Phoenixes and peonies: from a Nō theater jacket.

Butterflies, wild pinks, and balloon flowers: from a seventeenth-century Nō theater robe.

Morning glories, rose mallows, wild pinks, and bamboo leaves, with a geometric pattern: from a *yukata* (summer kimono).

Maple leaves on a geometric pattern: from a *yuzen* (printed silk) textile.

Camellias, balloon flowers, and maple leaves: from an embroidered textile.

Wisteria hat, wisteria, and weeping-cherry branches: from a kimono.

A Chinese lion, tree peonies, bamboo, and floral motifs:
from an eighteenth-century (mid Edo period) *yuzen* (printed silk) textile.

A crane; bamboo, pine, and mallow leaves (symbols of longevity):
from an eighteenth-century (mid Edo period) textile.

*Yuusoku* design: from a twelfth-century (Heian period) textile.

Fans and a wave motif: from a seventeenth-century (early Edo period) textile.

A bird, cherry blossoms, and a wave motif: from a nineteenth-century textile.

A flower cart with peonies and chrysanthemums; a butterfly; and a wave motif:
from a fifteenth-century (Muromachi period) embroidered textile.

Cranes, plums and plum blossoms, bamboo leaves, and a pine motif:
from an indigo-dyed *furoshiki* (wrapping cloth).

A crane, a tortoise, bamboo leaves, plums and plum blossoms, Japanese umbrella pines, and a wave motif (symbols of longevity): from a seventeenth-century (early Edo period) indigo-dyed textile.

15

Carp and a wave motif: from a stenciled textile.

Balls and chrysanthemums: from a nineteenth-century (early Meiji period) stenciled textile.

Japanese umbrella pine, wisteria, bamboo leaves, and a cherry-blossom motif:
from a *yuzen* (printed silk) textile.

Grapes and vine leaves: from eighteenth-century lacquerware.

Flower baskets and autumn creeping plants: from a stenciled textile.

Wild ducks, chrysanthemums, and cherry blossoms: from a *yuzen* (printed silk) textile.

Peonies, cherry blossoms, bamboo leaves, and a wave motif: from a *yuzen* (printed silk) textile.

A dragonfly and autumn blossoms: from lacquerware.

The moon, clouds, rabbits, and a wave motif: from a nineteenth-century ceramic.

Birds, plum blossoms, and plums: from a porcelain vase.

Morning glories and bamboo: from a *yukata* (summer kimono).

Autumn flower arrangements and a good-luck mallet: from a kimono.

Butterflies, chrysanthemums, Japanese apricots, and camellias: from lacquerware.

A pattern of fans with varied designs; autumn flowers: from a *yukata* (summer kimono).

Dragon and clouds: from a festival tapestry.